The Be-All End-All
Get Me A Job
Book

The Be-All End-All Get Me A Job Book

*350 Guaranteed to Work
Job Search Tips*

Kelly Barrington

McGraw-Hill, Inc.

New York   San Francisco   Washington, D.C.   Auckland   Bogotá
Caracas   Lisbon   London   Madrid   Mexico City   Milan
Montreal   New Delhi   San Juan   Singapore
Sydney   Tokyo   Toronto

Library of Congress Cataloging-in-Publication Data

Barrington, Kelly.
    The be-all, end-all, get me a job book : 350 guaranteed to work
  job search tips / Kelly Barrington.
        p.   cm.
    ISBN 0-07-005273-5
    1. Job hunting.   2. Resumes (Employment)   3. Vocational guidance.
  I. Title.
  HF5382.7.B373   1995
  650.14—dc20   95-9216
                                                                   CIP

1 2 3 4 5 6 7 8 9 0   DOC/DOC   9 0 0 9 8 7 6 5

ISBN 0-07-005273-5

*The sponsoring editor for this book was Betsy Brown, the editing supervisor was
Joseph Bertuna, and the production supervisor was Donald F. Schmidt. This book was
set in New Baskerville by Terry Leaden of McGraw-Hill's Professional Book Group
composition unit.*

Printed and bound by R. R. Donnelley & Sons Company.

McGraw-Hill books are available at special quantity discounts to use as premi-
ums and sales promotions, or for use in corporate training programs. For more
information, please write to the Director of Special Sales, McGraw-Hill, Inc.,
11 West 19th Street, New York, NY 10011. Or contact your local bookstore.

This publication is designed to provide accurate and authoritative information
in regard to the subject matter covered. It is sold with the understanding that
the publisher is not engaged in rendering legal, accounting, or other professional service. If legal advice or other expert assistance is required, the services
of a competent professional person should be sought.
                          —*from a declaration of principles jointly adopted by a committee
                            of the American Bar Association and a committee of publishers*

To my children, Ryan and Micaela, the wind beneath my wings and…

My mother, Edith Kelly, who always believed I had a story to tell
My father, Austin Kelly, who never gave in to defeat
My family and friends—Mikey, Lili, Jody, Nici, Eddie, Michael, Jennifer, Sue,
* Janet, Robin, Rob, Bill—for cheering me on*
My friends and mentors, Susan and M. J., for their words of wisdom
My best pal, Connie, for 15 years of wonderful irreverence
My bosses—Lee, Pamela, Frank, Alan, Gene, Cheryl—for honoring my creativity
My clients, for encouraging me to write this book for job seekers everywhere

Contents

It's Not Rocket Science   ix

Finding That Job: How to Get Started (Tip 1–51)   **1**

Putting First Things First: Self-Assessment (Tip 52–87)   **19**

Resumes That Sell (Tip 88–140)   **33**

Line Up Your References—Now (Tip 141–157)   **51**

Research, Research, Research (Tip 158–179)   **59**

Classified Ads: Where the Jobs Aren't (Tip 180–199)   **69**

What About Headhunters? (Tip 200–214)   **77**

Networking—People Power (Tip 215–237)   **85**

Interview Preparation—Do It! (Tip 238–264)   **95**

Interview Know-How (Tip 265–322)   **105**

Negotiating Your Package (Tip 323–343)   **125**

Parting Words (Tip 344–350)   **135**

It's Not Rocket Science

I didn't set out to write a book about how to get a job. It just happened. Over the past 15 years of recruiting, I've discovered a very interesting fact: Once someone knows what I do for a living—manage the recruitment function for a Fortune 200 international corporation— the questions begin. At parties, in the dentist's chair, at the grocery store, even at professional get-togethers!

"How do I write a resume that gets interviews?"

"What do I do if I want to change careers?"

"I don't know what I want to do. Can you help me?"

"Where are the jobs?"

"How do I research a company?"

"What should I wear to an interview?"

"What are the most common interview questions?"

"How do I explain I haven't worked in two years?"

"What's an interview like these days?"

"How do I negotiate a good salary package?"

It occurred to me that people are needlessly mystified by the job search process. Believe me, it's not rocket science. Granted, we're not born knowing how to get a job. So where do we get the information? Schools do a pretty good job of teaching us how to do a job, but how to get a job? Not so far. So we learn by doing. Sounds reasonable. But what if we've had the same job for a long time or haven't worked in several years or are just getting out of school or just don't feel very confident about our job search skills? Then what? We ask for help.

When I wrote *The Be-All End-All Get Me a Job Book,* I imagined you, the reader, sitting in front of me, asking me all sorts of questions about how to mount a successful job search campaign. I included everything I could think of at the time. But there's so much more; every job seeker out there has uncovered one or two better ways of waging battle in the job jungle of the nineties. That's how it works. You learn, you do, you relearn, you do again.

Looking for a job is a challenge. The process isn't mysterious and the odds aren't stacked against you. You're in the driver's seat from day one. You have the power to get any job you want, anywhere, anytime. Believe in yourself, apply the rules of the job game, and go out there and get 'em!

ABOUT THE AUTHOR

Kelly Barrington is recruiting manager for an international Fortune 200 corporation and a former headhunter, outplacement consultant, career counselor, and teacher. Kelly feels it's her mission in life to demystify the job search process by giving her readers the tools to get any job, anywhere, anytime, FAST!

Kelly is available for keynote speeches, seminars, and workshops. For further information or to share your own job search tips, contact:

KELLY BARRINGTON
P.O. Box 1637
Mill Valley, CA 94942

Finding That Job: How to Get Started

1. Job Search myth number 1: Good things come to those who wait. Probably not. Good things come to those who initiate. Don't sit around and expect a job to come to you. Make it happen—now!

2. The Job Game is a game of elimination. Like musical chairs, the winner is the one with the seat at the end. So don't get eliminated along the way. You want to make sure you're in the game long enough to get a job offer.

3. Is your goal to get any job offer? Probably not. What if the offer is to do something you hate 50 miles from home midnight to 8:00 a.m. for 50 percent less than what you're making now?

4. One job offer is not enough. Your goal should be to get multiple job offers—so you can choose the best one for you.

5. Never procrastinate when it comes to looking for a job. If you're working and feel it's time to leave, trust your instincts and start looking *now*.

6. Unemployed and want to take a month or two off? Don't do it! The longer you're out of the job market, the harder it is to find .

7. Fired? Laid off? Downsized? Displaced? Don't panic. Seventy percent of all job seekers find another job within six months, usually making more money to boot.

8. Good people are always in demand, regardless of the economy. Continuous self-improvement is the key. Keep your skills current, your resume updated, your network active.

9. Don't stay angry at your last employer. The longer you keep connected emotionally to the past, the harder it is to get on with your life. Success is the best revenge. Don't get even—get ahead.

10. Usually it's better not to waste time and energy on thoughts of litigation against your former employer. Move on.

11. There's no stigma associated with losing your job. It's happening to a lot more people now than ever before. So never, never be ashamed of it.

12. Don't be lulled into a false sense of security by big, fat severance packages. Over time, money runs out.

13. Don't go on vacation, rehab your house, or relax for a few months "to get your head together" right after you leave your job. Line up your new job now and negotiate a delayed start date instead. You'll feel a lot better.

14. But if you're really in shock after losing your job, take a couple of weeks off before plunging into your job search.

15. The best time to job hunt: mid-January through March and September through October. The worst times? Mid-November through New Year's.

16. Know thyself: What job or jobs you want, in what kinds of fields, industries, and companies? How can you get somewhere if you don't know where you want to go?

17. Don't know what you want to do? Pick 5 industries and 10 companies that really interest you—regardless of what field or job you're in now. Start gathering information about them. Read. Research. Talk to people. You may find a perfect fit.

18. Never listen to what other people say you should do for a living. It's *your* career. *You* decide.

19. Never buy into job search myths—overqualified, overeducated, over the hill. Companies need trained, experienced new hires who can hit the ground running. Let them know: They can't afford *not* to hire you.

20. Forget excuses like "I can't get a job because I'm over 50," "No one wants me because I'm hard of hearing," or "I don't stand a chance as a woman in this male-dominated industry." Employers want qualified candidates, regardless of age, race, gender, or disabilities. Talent triumphs.

21. Employers hire qualified candidates. Be honest. Are you the most marketable you can be?

22. Be proactive. Jobs don't come looking for you the way they did 10 or 15 years ago. *You* have to find them by asking questions, doing research, networking with everyone you know.

23. Hustle is the name of the game. Unless you're devoting 40 hours a week to looking for a job, you're not a serious job seeker.

24. Never rule out temporary work. It's a great way to shop for interesting companies, industries, and fields without any obligation to buy.

25. Consult. Companies are outsourcing everything from payroll to programming to advertising. Going in as an independent contractor can be a great way to get your foot in the door.

26. Never turn down a chance to volunteer. It's a brilliant way to meet new people and network. Volunteering also helps you build new skills that can make you more attractive to employers.

27. Put yourself on a budget immediately if you're about to be out of work. Expect to be unemployed six months and plan accordingly. Know your fixed expenses.

28. Don't punish yourself by cutting out a favorite activity, hobby, or pastime. You need balance to stay positive. Moderation is the name of the game.

29. Mortgage or credit card worries because you're out of work? Call your creditors and make them partners in your job search—now.

30. Fear of foreclosure? Banks don't want to foreclose on you. They'll work with you, but don't wait until you're three months behind in payments. Let them know before there's a problem.

31. You may be unemployed six months or more depending upon where you live, type of job, salary, age, and experience. Don't make any major purchase until you've secured your next job.

32. Limited resources? There may be gold in your possessions. Have a garage sale, sell old "valuables," unload the second car.

33. Realize there's grief associated with job loss and get help if you need it. If family and friends aren't enough, contact local self-help groups or church groups for referrals. You need to deal with your grief *now* so you can move on.

34. Even when you're out of work get lots of exercise, eat right, maintain social contacts, and pursue hobbies. A balanced life puts you in the right frame of mind to job search successfully.

35. Job search myth number 2: It's easier to find a job when you have a job. Wrong! When will you have time to answer ads, network, talk to recruiters, research, and interview? Looking for a job is a full-time job.

36. For every $10,000 in annual salary, it takes one month of dedicated, 40-hour-a-week job search to secure your next job.

37. Set up a home office as your command post and stock it with adequate supplies, including a computer and answering machine. (You'll need to produce high-quality cover letters and resumes.)

38. Computer-phobic? Take classes immediately. You must be PC-literate to compete in the 1990s.

39. Always be organized. Maintain files of all companies you're interested in, ads you've responded to, letters you've written.

40. Keep track of everyone you talk to—name, date, title, phone number, reason for call, disposition, when to call back. It's critical to track your activity.

41. Get an answering machine or service with remote capabilities so you can access your messages when you're not at home.

42. Never let anyone—especially children—answer your home phone but you. You want to make sure *you* get your messages.

43. Record a brief, businesslike message on your answering machine—nothing hip, gimmicky, sexy, or sentimental. And no music. Remember, you never get a second chance to make a first impression. Recruiters don't call twice.

44. Retrieve your messages frequently and return calls promptly. Good follow-through is an essential part of any job and critical to the job search process. Show the world you're on top of things.

45. Keep your spirits up. People like people who are upbeat, optimistic, positive. Even if you feel down, don't give in to negativism. By acting upbeat, you'll soon feel "up."

46. One way to stay positive: Make copies of all the nice things people have written about you—customer letters, performance appraisals, awards. Tape them to your mirror. Read them every morning and night and remember how good you really are.

47. Never be ashamed to stand in the unemployment line. It's your money. You've earned it. It's available to help your transition to your next job.

48. Networking on the unemployment line? It's really possible! Your local unemployment office is a great place to meet people, share job leads, and get support.

49. Looking for a job when you're still working? It's tricky. Be careful of noticeable changes in your normal pattern. Don't take extra time off, come to work dressed better than usual, increase or decrease the amount of work you do, or go low profile if you've always been high profile.

50. Job in jeopardy? It is if you've been cut out of the loop, that is, not invited to meetings or not put on key committees. So act now. You want to leave on your terms, not theirs.

51. Interviewing begins the moment you have any contact with a potential employer—whether via your resume, a telephone call, or a face-to-face meeting. Always put your best face forward and never let your guard down.

Putting First Things First: Self-Assessment

52. Ask: Who am I? What do I want out of life? A job? A career? Where am I going? Do I know how to get there? Have I been happy in my work/career/profession? What would I like to change?

53. Always take a personal inventory. What do I like? What am I good at? What kinds of people do I like to work with? What industries interest me? Ask lots of questions. The answers will lead you to your next job.

54. Be aware of what the marketplace wants. Read. Research. Ask questions. What are the hot industries, fields, and companies in your area? Who's hiring? Who's laying off? How do you fit in the new job market?

55. List three things you liked about each of your last
    three jobs. Look for common threads. Try to
    repeat these in your next job.

56. *Skills sell.* Make a list of the things you know how to do really well. They are the keys to your next job.

57. While job hunting take a class or go to school at night. The more skills you have, the more employable you are. Schools are great places to network, too.

58. Think "currentcy"—current skills translate into salary dollars. Stay on the cutting edge in your field. You're only as good as your marketable skills.

59. Imagine you're a product and you're taking that product to market. Why should a company "buy" your product? What makes you unique, special, different?

60. Can you list your own features and benefits? You'll need to "sell" them in an interview.

61. Identify your needs. What's important to you? Power? Status? Money? Creativity? Teamwork? Autonomy?

62. Know the competition. How do you compare with your peers in education, experience, training, salary, career progression? Hot products move. Are you new and improved or just the same old, same old.

63. Learn to toot your own horn. Time yourself five minutes and write down every compliment you've received on the job, formal (performance appraisal) or informal. (You'll be surprised how terrific you really are!)

64. Recruiters care about two things—credentials and personality. Can you do the job based on past performance and will you fit in with the corporate culture?

65. Personality is important. List three of your positive personality traits (for example, dependable, friendly, resourceful), then give an example of how you demonstrate each trait on the job. How you act is as important as what you can do.

66. Past performance is the best indicator of future performance. If you were successful at one company, odds are you can succeed at another.

67. Focus your effort. The shotgun approach to job seeking is too scattered. Target specific fields, industries, and companies for your job search; then take aim and fire.

68. Always plan ahead. Plan A is landing the optimal job that meets all of your requirements—money, duties, location, etc. Plans B and C are your fall-back positions.

69. Execute Plan A for the first one to two months. Then go right into Plan B. Remember, your next job will most likely not be your last anyway.

70. Is self-employment for you?

71. Maybe you should go back to school for more training, to finish a degree, to pick up another one.

72. No money for school? Visit the financial aid office of your local college or junior college to inquire about grants, low-interest student loans, or scholarships.

73. Haven't the foggiest idea what you want to do? Go to the career placement office of your local junior college for low-cost, sometimes free, career testing or assessment.

74. Honor your values and priorities. If family time is important to you, don't consider jobs with overtime, heavy travel, or demanding work schedules. Never lose sight of your priorities in life.

75. Research the market and know the salary range for your particular field, industry, level of expertise. Use the library. Ask colleagues. Call your professional association.

76. The last word on salary—you're worth as much as you say you're worth.

77. Make the business section of the library your second home.

78. Don't get hung up on fancy job titles, big corporate names, glitzy fields, glamorous industries. You want a job that pays you well to do the work you enjoy. Period.

79. Don't hang onto the glamour and status of your old company. There are plenty of great companies out there that thrive in obscurity. Glamour and status don't pay the rent.

80. Look for a job that makes you happy. Start noticing what interests you, excites you, makes you smile.

81. Visualize success. See yourself in your new job, making the salary you deserve, working with people you like and respect, doing interesting work, being happy.

82. Re-engineer yourself. New products sell. Old products don't. Investigate a new hairstyle, cut, or color. Look progressive.

83. Dress to impress. Invest in an interview wardrobe. You'll need more than one outfit since you'll interview more than once at any given company.

84. Get feedback from friends and colleagues on your body language, appearance, voice, posture.

85. First impressions are lasting impressions. Spend as much as you can on high-quality interview clothes, including shoes and briefcase. Opt for stylish, tailored designs in neutral business colors. And go easy on the jewelry.

86. Success sells. Know your past achievements, triumphs, accomplishments. Be prepared to toot your own horn.

87. Life is dealing you a new hand. One closed door often leads to another open door. Be open to all the possibilities: New field, industry, location, structure, environment, culture, people.

Resumes That Sell

88. A resume won't get you a job. But a resume will get you an interview, so sweat it a little, knowing you can always revise it if you need to.

89. A resume is a snapshot of your career, nothing more. It's one-dimensional. Like a photograph it doesn't smile, gesture, talk, or move. But every word, line, and phrase yells who you are loud and clear.

90. Have someone in your field critique your resume before you send it out. Does it sell your unique talents and abilities?

91. Short resumes get read. Long resumes get filed. Keep it brief, snappy, easy to read, to the point. And don't go back more than 10 years. That's ancient history.

92. Remember the five-second rule: If your resume doesn't grab the reader in the first five seconds, it won't get read.

93. Make your resume easy on the eyes. Put company names, job titles, and dates of employment in bold capital letters.

94. Should you use a chronological or a functional format? Choose chronological. Recruiters wonder what you've got to hide by using the functional format.

95. Never use "curriculum vitae." It's pretentious.

96. Also pretentious: The fold-out "Presentation of Qualifications" on parchment paper and the word "resume" spelled with an accent on the "e."

97. White space on a resume is important. Leave big margins on all sides and lots of white space in the middle. The average recruiter reads hundreds of resumes a month. Make yours easy to read.

98. Resume dropouts: over two pages in length, small size font, unusual paper color or stock.

99. A salute to English teachers everywhere: You were right. Grammar and spelling *are* important. Even one error will place your resume in the "thanks but no thanks" pile. Who wants an employee with no attention to detail?

100. What's wrong with a little white lie? If it's on your resume, everything. NEVER LIE! That's why references were invented.

101. So you didn't graduate from college or get an MBA. So what? A good work history speaks louder than a couple of degrees.

102. So you're 40-plus, who cares? Employers do. Companies today want skilled, trained workers. In your job search, emphasize experience.

103. The more experience you have, the less important the degree. Most employers today want new hires who can be productive from day one.

104. Never fudge on dates or fake degrees. These are career killers.

105. Gaps in employment? It doesn't have to be a problem. Just be prepared to explain why you were out of work.

106. Resumes are meant to be brief. They are a snapshot of your credentials. It should leave the reader wanting to know more about you, not less.

107. Write in phrases, not sentences. Imagine your resume is an urgent telegram. What information is absolutely crucial for the reader to know about you?

108. Don't let your ego get in the way of writing a winning resume. Detach. Remain objective. And revise your resume at least five times until it works.

109. Avoid pronouns like "I." The reader assumes you did all the things you say you did on the resume.

110. Tantalize. Generalize. Give overviews. Allude to much, much more. If your resume lists everything you've ever done in your career, the reader will assume that whatever is left out you haven't done.

111. Success sells. Emphasize your accomplishments, triumphs, achievements. Anyone can perform a job; it's *how* you performed that makes you attractive to the next employer.

112. Think action. Express accomplishments with action verbs like "achieved," "created," "earned," "developed."

113. Avoid weak verbs like "helped," "assisted," "participated in." These words minimize one's contributions.

114. A resume is a direct-mail piece. It needs to sell. If your phone's ringing off the hook, it's working. If it's not, revise it— now.

115. Don't include graduation dates unless you're a recent graduate. Dates reveal age, and age shouldn't matter. Let the recruiter see you first before making a judgment on your talents and abilities.

116. Jobless at 50? You have experience to sell. Capitalize on chronology.

117. Just graduating or a recent graduate? Emphasize *any* experience that can be applied to a real job (summer jobs as a clerk at a law firm, editor of school newspaper, treasurer of student activity club).

118. You should never include irrelevant personal information like age (taboo), marital or health status (does a sick person ever admit to it in writing?), height, weight, number of children (who cares?).

119. Never include salary information in your resume or cover letter.

120. Salary negotiation rule of thumb: Whoever mentions money first loses. Don't show your hand until the employer loves you and wants to hire you.

121. Don't use a resume service to write your resume. You'll get better results—and save a lot of money—if you do it yourself. Canned resumes are a turnoff.

122. Don't use gimmicks or try to be "cute."
Recruiters have seen it all—resumes on oversized
paper, in cans, on boxes, in telegrams, delivered
via singing messengers.

123. Pictures on your resume? Never. You're looking
for a job, not entering a beauty contest (unless
you're looking for an acting or modeling job).

124. Have your resume professionally printed on a
laser printer using high-quality bond paper.
Never photocopy. In preparing a resume,
presentation is everything.

125. Use your resume as a networking device. Show it
to friends and business associates. Ask them to
pass it on as appropriate. Give them extra copies
just in case.

126. Mass mailings don't work. They are expensive and ineffective. Direct mail yields a 1 to 2 percent response, tops. And most of the response will be "thanks but no thanks" postcards from busy personnel departments.

127. Don't send a resume without a cover letter— ever. The reader needs to know why you're sending a resume. Were you referred by someone? Is this in response to an ad? Are you fishing?

128. Always send your cover letter and resume to the person who can hire you. Bypass personnel at all costs. They're a screening mechanism. Go to the top if you want results.

129. Never send your cover letter and resume to a title like "Marketing Manager" or "Finance Department." These letters get routed to Personnel or to the wastepaper basket.

130.   Your cover letter must be perfect—no spelling errors, punctuation goofs, grammar gaffes. So read it twice before you mail it.

131. Check and recheck the spelling of the names of the company and the manager. Never misspell the name of the recipient.

132. If you're responding to a classified ad, say so and indicate the name of the newspaper and the date the ad ran. Recruiters always track newspaper results.

133. Forget humor in cover letters and resumes. Save the comedy for after you get the job.

134. Avoid using such saintly qualities as "honest" and "sincere."

135. Not sure of how to address the letter? Some first names can be non–gender specific. Always call the company and asks if it's Mr. or Ms. Get the gender right.

136. Put your return address on all correspondence, just in case.

137. Unlike personnel managers, hiring managers don't read zillions of resumes a month. They're more likely to read and respond to your resume. And they'll be impressed by your resourcefulness.

138. Your cover letter should be short and to the point. Two to three paragraphs is best. Close by telling the reader you'll follow up within a week. That way when the secretary asks "Is Mr. Jones expecting your call?" you can say "yes."

139. Your resume should get at least one response from 10 to 15 mailings. If not, redo it.

140. Good resumes are gold. Once you have a good resume, update it yearly. Keep it fresh.

Line Up Your Your References —Now

141. References can make or break you. Contact them before you need them. Get work and home numbers. Always ask, "Can I count on you to give me a good reference?"

142. Prepare your references. Review with them key information: your dates of service, title, duties, accomplishments, strengths. Always confirm salary.

143. Create your own reference statement, including key information, and send it to your references in advance. Make sure your stories match.

144.   Feed your references one weakness that's really a strength in disguise, something like "She overcommitted herself on several projects and wound up working a lot of overtime." Never leave it up to your references to think of a real weakness.

145. Don't burn bridges. You'll need former employers and bosses as references. Leave graciously, even if involuntarily. Show them what a professional you really are and that's how they'll remember you.

146. Make sure at least one reference is an ex-supervisor, but never use anyone who might give you a bad reference.

147. Forget personal references. Employers want to know how you performed on the job from the manager who supervised you.

148. Are you a recent graduate? Use professors to supplement business references.

149. Fired? Get a letter of recommendation from your boss. You want to know what he's going to say about you before he says it.

150. Relieved you have letters of reference? Not so fast. Recruiters will call your references anyway even if you have letters of reference from these people.

151. Remember the mall rule: Your ex-boss wants you to get another job because he's afraid of running into you at the mall when you're still unemployed. A complimentary reference will soothe his conscience.

152. Never include references on your resume.

153. Downsized? Save newspaper articles and press releases to substantiate your reason for departure come reference time.

154. Contact your references when you're about to get an offer and prepare them for the reference call. They'll appreciate the thoughtfulness.

155. When employers check references, they're looking for confirmation of what they already believe about you. So coach your references.

156. Let your references know if you got the job. Drop them a note thanking them for their help. Being gracious pays off.

157. Keep in touch with your references after you start your new job. Send them your business card. Include them on your holiday card list. Keep them in your network. You never know when you may need them again.

Research,
Research,
Research

158. The person with the best information wins. Research every company, industry, field, and location you're interested in. Be the resident expert.

159. *Caveat emptor*—let the buyer beware. If you take a job and later find out the company's in trouble, you have only yourself to blame. Look before you leap.

160. Make friends with your local librarian. Libraries are great storehouses of information. Learn how to use Infotrac, a data retrieval software program, to source current information on companies.

161. Visit your library regularly and park yourself in the business section. Read all the business periodicals to stay current on business events and trends.

162. Maintain research files on companies, fields, industries of interest. If the company is publicly held, call the company's investor relations department and get an annual report and any other available information.

163. Current information is the best information. Annual reports are fine, but the real lowdown on a company is found in newspapers, business magazines, trade publications.

164. Keep a file on every company you research and fill it with articles, Dun & Bradstreet/Moody's reports, and general information. You'll need it later for the interview.

165. You want to make sure there are no skeletons in the closet of a prospective employer—like a possible takeover, shaky financials, poor senior management, threatening litigation.

166. If the company is local, visit the corporate office and ask for the information in person. You may get material not commonly sent out. You'll also get a chance to demonstrate just how resourceful you are.

167.	What are the fastest-growing companies in your area? These companies may not advertise openings, but they're hiring.

168.	Be a research junkie. Read everything you can lay your hands on. Stay current. Know what's going on.

169.	Opportunities are everywhere. A change in senior management spells personnel changes down the road. New management wants new blood. Learn to read between the lines and anticipate openings.

170.	New management at one company points to openings at another. The new guy had to come from somewhere. Call to find out if that position has been filled.

171.   Think hot industries: telecommunications, tourism, entertainment, personal services, multimedia, educational software, nonprofit, legal services, information services, healthcare, biotech, environmental, waste management, education, training.

172.   Think major social trends: aging population, education crisis, healthcare crisis, technology revolution, multiculturalism, women in the work force, rise in crime, homelessness. Trends mean opportunities.

173.   Devour the business section of your local newspaper(s) every day for news on local businesses. Read *The Wall Street Journal, Fortune, Forbes,* and *Business Week* for the big picture.

174. At least once, spend an hour with *The Dictionary of Occupational Titles*. You'll get a mind-blowing trip through 30,000-plus job titles organized by career families. The possibilities for jobs are endless.

175. Research job hot-line numbers. Most big companies and many professional associations have prerecorded employment hot lines that list job opportunities. Take advantage of this free service.

176. Visit the Career Placement Center of your local college and/or junior college. They have a good reference section on local employers with job postings to boot.

177. Don't forget your greatest resource for insider information—current or past colleagues, vendors, service providers. Ask everyone you know for information. You may be surprised by who knows what.

178. Always know how much you're worth in the marketplace. Check it out with professional associations, classified ads, even colleagues. You may be surprised.

179. What to research? Everything. Industry/market trends, number of years in business, annual revenues for past five years, products/services, management changes, competitors, future plans.

Classified Ads: Where the Jobs Aren't

180. Classified ads account for only about 5 percent of job openings, so don't spend all of your time answering ads.

181. Devote Sundays to answering ads and planning your strategy for the next week. Don't spend precious weekday hours behind a computer. You need to be out there sourcing leads, networking, interviewing.

182. Read the classifieds from A to Z. Job titles vary from company to company. An administrative assistant at one company might be an information specialist at another.

183. Companies running multiple ads are hiring in general. Send your resume and cover letter to the head of the department you want to work in and indicate you heard there may be an opening.

184. Always address correspondence to the person who has the authority to hire you.

185. Read the classifieds for information on what's hot, what's not. Be an avid classifieds reader and find out who's hiring, for what jobs, at what salaries.

186. Keep a copy of every ad you respond to and every letter you write. If the company calls you, you want to know what you said and why.

187.   Be prepared for telephone interviews. They can come unexpectedly and suddenly. So keep your ad file and resume by the phone.

188.   Don't be surprised if a recruiter calls you at night or on the weekends.

189.   Proofread all correspondence. Spelling and grammatical errors don't fly in corporations. What a shame it would be to be disqualified for poor attention to detail.

190. Apply for every job you're interested in, whether or not you meet all the requirements. Ad copy is a wish list. Employers often don't expect to get everything they ask for.

191. Don't let the lack of a degree get in your way.
      You're the sum total of all of your experiences.

192. Dig deeper in the classifieds and learn the
      jargon, skill set, and educational requirements
      for most jobs, fields, industries.

193. Bypass Personnel. Their job is to screen you out.
      And they're usually the last to know about an
      opening.

194. Go to the top. Most unsolicited resumes to
      senior executives get read. Generally, the bigger
      they are, the more approachable they are.

195. No response to your resume and cover letter? It
      doesn't hurt to reapply for the same job.
      Resumes get lost, misfiled, routed.

196.   The best day for classifieds in your local paper is Sunday. *The Wall Street Journal* features ads in its Monday, Tuesday, and Wednesday editions. *The National Business Employment Weekly* features ads for jobs all across the United States. Be sure and check out the ads in trade publications and association newsletters also.

197.   Beware of blind ads. Companies run blind ads for a variety of reasons. Respond to ones that interest you but be careful, especially if you're still working. You could be responding to your own company.

198.   Thinking about relocation? Read the Sunday papers of the cities you're interested in. Most big libraries subscribe to major metropolitan newspapers.

199. Want to work abroad? The "International Jobs" section of *The National Business Employment Weekly* carries the best leads on international jobs.

What About Headhunters?

200. Headhunters are paid matchmakers. They make money putting companies and candidates together. But never forget who they work for. (Not you. They're paid by the employer.)

201. Headhunters are working for you in the negotiation process. Since their fee is a percentage of your first year's salary, they'll try to negotiate the best package possible for you.

202. Don't be intimidated by headhunters and executive recruiters. Never let them railroad you into a job that doesn't meet your criteria.

203. Research the best headhunters in your field, then send them a resume and cover letter. Follow up with a phone call and press for an interview, however brief. You must get a face-to-face.

204. Cultivate long-term relationships with headhunters in your field. They can make or break your career. Call periodically, send cards, mail interesting newspaper articles. Stay connected.

205. Headhunters tend to specialize. So look in the yellow pages under Employment Agencies and/or Executive Search Firms to find recruiters/headhunters in your location who specialize in your field or industry.

206. Never go around a headhunter to get to the hiring manager. Try it and they'll cut you out of the loop faster than you can say "Hasta la vista, baby."

207. Headhunters are very image-conscious. Dress to impress. Remember you never get a second chance to make a first impression. Dress one to two levels above your position.

208. Search firms and employment agencies aren't charitable organizations. They're only interested in you if they can place you. They won't shop you around until they have a buyer.

209. Agency versus search firm? An employment agency usually works on jobs $50,000 and below in annual salary; a search firm works on jobs above $50,000, many over $100,000.

210. Never sign anything. You may be liable for a fee! Most agencies are Fee Paid by Employer, but some agencies are Fee Paid by Employee. That's you! Be wary.

211. Never agree to an exclusive relationship with one recruiter. Maximize your exposure. Use two or three.

212. Don't count on headhunters exclusively to get you a job. Agencies and search firms generally account for only 10 to 15 percent of all jobs filled. So be proactive. Do your research. Source leads. Talk to everyone.

213. Rule of thumb: The higher the salary of the job you're looking for, the more important a headhunter is to your job search success. At salaries over $100,000, they're responsible for over 50 percent of all placements.

214. Job hunting can involve a long series of rejections. Don't fear rejection. Celebrate it. In salesperson's terms, each "no" brings you that much closer to "yes."

Networking —People Power

215. Job search myth number 3: Networking is asking people for a job. Wrong. Networking is asking others for advice. Asking for a job makes people feel uncomfortable. Asking for help makes people feel valued.

216. Most of the available jobs are in the hidden job market. They aren't listed in the classifieds or placed with a headhunter. Find them through your network of contacts.

217. Everyone you know is a contact. The average person knows dozen of people you don't know. Build your network of contacts.

218. An easy way to develop a list of contacts: Get a piece of paper and pen. Time yourself 10 minutes. Then write down the first names of every adult you know, working or not. You'll be surprised how many people you really know. This is your network.

219. Your network leads to other networks. People *you know* are primary contacts. People you're referred to by people you know are secondary contacts. Both are helpful sources of information.

220. People to network with: friends, relatives, neighbors, colleagues, former co-workers, club members, and members of religious affiliations.

221. Don't assume the little old lady who lives next door who hasn't worked for 30 years can't help you. How do you know whom she knows? Ask.

222. It's not who you know but who you are willing to know. Become active in professional, social, civic organizations. Meet as many people as you can and get the word out.

223.   Looking for a job is a numbers game. The more contacts you make, the more interviews you'll get. The more interviews you have, the more offers you'll get.

224. Don't mistake networking for singing the blues about your last employer. This is not the time to rail against your misfortune. Networking is about the future, not the past.

225. Get your story straight. People can't help you if you don't give them the proper information. Know what you want in your next job before you start networking.

226. Prepare a 60-second networking pitch. Explain why you left your last job, what kind of job you're looking for, in what kinds of industries. Then clarify with examples by listing five companies you'd like to work for.

227. Try to network face to face, not over the phone. You'll get more buy-in with the personal touch. Ask for just 10 minutes of your contact's time, then stick to it.

228. Pick their brain. Whom do they know who might be able to help you? Where could you go for more information? Do they have any ideas?

229. Live on the phone during your job search. Call everyone you know. Telemarket.

230. Telephone tag doesn't fly in job search. People won't try too hard to call you back. Don't leave a message. Keep calling until you reach the person directly.

231.   Work that room. Network at professional get-togethers: lunches, breakfast meetings, dinners, after-hours mixers, seminars, trade shows.

232.   Hand out a business card with your name, phone number, and field or area of specialization on it. It works.

233.   Turned down for a job? Use the interviewer as a networking contact. Interviewers may know of similar openings at other companies.

234.   Keep track of your network. Note the name of each contact, phone numbers, title, company, date, and disposition. Were there referrals? Suggestions? When should you check back with them?

235. Nurture your network. Send birthday, anniversary, get well, holiday cards. Keep in touch, especially when you don't need them. People like to feel needed, not used.

236. The higher you are on the corporate ladder, the more you need to network. The old boy/girl network is alive and well. Use it.

237. Don't forget to network with other job seekers. They're a tremendous source of information about specific industries and companies. They're out there doing battle, just like you.

Interview Preparation —Do It!

238. Interviewing is 90 percent preparation and 10 percent application. So prepare and you'll feel more relaxed, confident, and on top of things during the interview.

239. Review and role-play the most frequently asked questions. Prepare your answers to questions like: Why are you leaving your job? Why are you interested in this position? What do you know about our company?

240. Have answers to the questions that make you squirm. Why were you terminated? Why do you have gaps in employment? Why did you stay at your last company so long? Do you have a degree?

241. What about personal questions concerning marital status, number of children, health? Try to figure out the underlying concern. For example, the question "What are your child-care arrangements?" might address the availability to travel or work weekends. Answer the *real* question: "I will do whatever it takes to get the job done." Magic words: "You can count on me."

242. Before an interview, review your successes. What were they? How did you make them happen? What achievement are you proudest of? Can you tell them in 60 seconds or less?

243. Prepare your sales pitch. Know what the company is looking for and match your skills and background to the job requirements.

244. Practice your answers in front of the mirror, into a tape recorder, and on video, if possible. Look for nervous mannerisms like hair twirling, ear pulling, neck scratching.

245. Check your posture, eye contact, energy level. Evaluate your voice. Is it high and screeching? Are your answers punctuated with a lot of "er's" and "um's"?

246. For every interview, have at least five questions to ask the interviewer at the end of the interview. Examples : Why is this job open? What are you looking for in a successful candidate? What do you expect the new hire to accomplish in the first 90 days? Six months?

247. Important interview props—paper and pen. On the pad of paper include your five interview questions along with any major points about your background you want to cover in the interview.

248. Always bring samples of your work: press clippings of appearances or speeches, a quote by you in local publications, writing samples, etc. Interviewers love to see tangible evidence of your work. Be prepared to leave the samples with the interviewer, but never be afraid to ask for them back.

249. Assemble your research on the company. In a file, put information on the company's history, management, culture, financial condition, employment patterns, market position, current/future problems. This is evidence number 1.

250. Make a file of your accomplishments. Include any performance appraisals, letters of recommendation, complimentary letters, company newsletters with your name in them, reports or projects you've done. This is evidence number 2.

251. Evidence is critical to the interview. People believe what they see. Be prepared to show them what you've done, both in accomplishments and research. Evidence impresses.

252. First rule of interviewing: Make sure your shoes are polished and your heels are not worn.

253. Go on a reconnaissance mission. Visit the interview location before the interview to minimize the risk of getting lost, arriving late, or dressing inappropriately.

254. When in Rome...Notice how people are dressed in the building. Conservatively? Informally? Fashionably? Expensively? Plan your interview attire accordingly. Dress for your audience.

255. Get the inside scoop. Try to talk to someone who has first-hand information on the company—an employer, ex-employer, vendor, competitor.

256. Practice a firm handshake. First impressions are lasting ones. A damp, limp, tentative handshake spells trouble for any candidate. And please, no finger-to-finger handshakes.

257. Get a haircut before you go on any major interview.

258. Invest in quality clothes for the interview and make sure your grooming is impeccable. Hair must be neat, nails manicured, shoes polished. No exceptions.

259. Glasses? Yes. You can't risk poor vision in an interview.

260. Tinted lenses? No. If the tint's too dark, you'll look unprofessional.

261. Tone down makeup and jewelry. If it jangles or dangles, don't wear it. And skip the perfume and aftershave. Some people have fragrance allergies.

262. Men's interview uniform: Conservative suit in dark colors with a white dry-cleaned shirt. Ties are another story. An expensive, fashionable tie shows you're progressive, up-to-the-minute.

263. Women's interview uniform: Conservative suit or dress with jacket in dark or neutral colors. Red is also acceptable. Dark or neutral hose. Avoid faddish styles and hemlines.

264.   Critique your interview outfit. Does it make you look successful, competent, with it? Get feedback from friends and relatives. Clothes can tell a lot about you. Make sure they don't lie.

Interview Know-How

265. Fear of interviewing? Practice makes perfect. You'll get better over time.

266. An interview is a dialogue between two people. What you give is what you get. So be proactive. Ask questions and initiate discussion.

267. Confirm your interview time, date, and location one day in advance. Use this as a way to connect with your contact who could provide additional last-minute information.

268. NEVER be late to an interview.

269. If you are going to be late, call and reschedule instead. You'll make a much better impression being on time.

270. Bring extra copies of your resume with you. Never assume the interviewer can find your resume.

271. Arrive 15 minutes early and retire to the restroom. Check your appearance in the mirror. Hair in place? Makeup intact? Hose crisis? Women should pack an extra pair, just in case.

272. Introduce yourself to the secretary and be seated. (Secretaries are often hidden power bases, so engage them in conversation.)

273. Take off your coat and hang it up before the interview. In tennis shoes? Change into good shoes *before* you enter the building.

274. Look busy. Take out reading material on the company or peruse company literature available in the reception area while you wait. Don't fidget.

275. Some companies require all applicants to fill out an application, regardless of position. Fill it out completely, even if you have a resume.

276. Stand up to greet the interviewer and extend your hand. Give a firm handshake, but don't crush. And don't pump your arm up and down.

277. Once in the interviewer's office, wait to be seated. You don't want to sit in the interviewer's favorite chair.

278. Even if offered, don't smoke, chew gum, eat, or drink coffee during the interview. And don't eat garlic or drink alcohol before the interview.

279. Be observant. Are there pictures on the desk? Who's in the pictures? Trophies, awards? For what? Art? What kind? Be aware for small talk later on.

280. In an interview, be careful not to dwell on your personal life. If asked, be brief but polite. Remember, the interview is about what you can do on the job, not at home.

281. Don't name-drop, especially with a recruiter. If you know someone important, say so. But make sure there really is a connection. Recruiters have heard it all.

282. Never argue. If the interviewer says something you disagree with, let it go. This isn't a debate. It's an interview.

283. Answer only the questions asked. Be direct. Don't ramble. And never volunteer information.

284. Be brief. The more you try to embellish your answers, the more likely you are to say something that disqualifies you.

285. The earlier it is in the interview, the shorter your answers need to be. The interviewer has limited time and a list of questions to ask you.

286. Never take anyone with you to the interview. Go alone.

287. Don't assume the interviewer is knowledgeable about your industry, field, or specialty. Don't use jargon, company lingo, industry buzz words.

288. Be a good listener. Listen actively by nodding your head in agreement/acknowledgment. Lean forward to let the interviewer know you're interested.

289. Maintain good eye contact. Eyes averted spell lack of self-confidence, nervousness, insecurity.

290. Watch your body language. Don't fidget, cross your arms, slouch. Remember, everything you say and do broadcasts who you are.

291. Be enthusiastic, upbeat. Show your excitement for the job and company. Bring out your evidence file and share your company research with the interviewer.

292. Never ask about salary or benefits in the first interview. Save those issues for the negotiation session. You want the company to fall in love with you first.

293. Whoever mentions money first loses. If asked your salary requirements, respond with "What is the range for this position?" If pressed, give a broad range, but never a specific amount.

294. An interview is a dialogue between two people. Don't let the interviewer ramble or get sidetracked. Put your two cents in.

295. Control the interview by asking questions. People feel compelled to answer.

296. Be able to explain in two to three sentences what your job duties were. Keep it simple and basic.

297. Be able to explain in two to three sentences why you're looking for a job. Laid off? Downsized? Resigned? Why?

298. Never assume the interviewer knows what's been going on at your company. Explain why you left, but be brief.

299. Interview rule number 1: Never say anything negative about your company, your boss, your job, your colleagues, yourself.

300. Research pays off. Not knowing anything about the company interviewing you will hurt your chances of being hired.

301. Personality and intelligence can compensate for lack of specific job experience. Radiate self-confidence, enthusiasm, congeniality.

302. An interview is a sales pitch. Be prepared to sell your features and benefits. Why should they hire you? Make yourself irresistible.

303. Never show confidential documents or memos from your previous employer(s). No one wants to hire someone who steals company property.

304. Stumped for an answer to a tough question? Take time to collect your thoughts before you speak. Guard against babbling.

305. Don't be afraid to say "I don't know." Then add, "Would you rephrase the question?" Honesty wins points.

306. An interviewer cares about three things: Can you do the job (experience, education)? Will you do the job (hours, money, location)? and Will you fit in the company (personality)?

307. Remember people's names. Use last names unless the interviewer indicates you by your first name.

308. Past performance is the best indication of future performance. If you performed miracles for your last employer, you can do it again. So capitalize on your successes.

309. Don't interrupt. Some interviewers talk more than they listen. That's OK. Be a good listener.

310. Ask for business cards of everyone you talk to in the interview process. This is critical for follow-up thank-you letters, future networking calls, general job search record keeping.

311. Interviewing rule of thumb: It takes 10 to 15 networking contacts to generate one interview and 5 to 10 interviews to generate one offer.

312. Rejection is tough, but don't take it personally. Detach. It's just business. After each rejection, evaluate why. Then figure out what you can do in the future to avoid the same thing happening again.

313. Never leave an interview without thanking the interviewer and going for the trial close. Ask, "What's the next step? Where do we go from here?"

314. Anyone's worst nightmare—a group interview. Relax. Don't panic. Direct your answers to the person asking the most questions but maintain eye contact with everyone.

315. A lunch interview? Order something easy to eat. Always graciously decline alcoholic beverages, even if the interviewer indulges. And mind your manners.

316. If the interviewer keeps you waiting for more than 30 minutes, reschedule. You'll both feel better meeting under different circumstances.

317. Fear of shrinking? Don't make an issue out of taking psychological tests. They're no big deal, and many companies use them, both pre- and postemployment.

318. Don't be intimidated by interviewers, especially personnel types. They want you to be the right candidate. It makes their job easier.

319. Assess how you did after the interview. Did you babble, evade questions, fidget, reveal too much? Learn from your mistakes, but don't be too hard on yourself. You're learning how to interview.

320. Write thank-you notes immediately. Be brief, but gracious. This is a courtesy note only. Resist going in for the kill with a final sales pitch.

321. Don't use "Thank-You" stationery or stationery with business letterheads. And never send humorous cards.

322.   The next time you make a job move for money,
        take this test: divide the difference between your
        old salary and your new salary by 12; take about
        35 to 40 percent off for taxes and deductions.
        That's how much more you're going to take
        home each month. Then ask: is making the
        move worth it?

Negotiating Your Package

323. You don't have to accept the first salary offer. You can negotiate.

324. When negotiating your salary, think in terms of the entire compensation package: salary, bonus, commissions, tuition assistance, car, expenses, title, workweek, hours.

325. Identify what's important to you right now. Money? Hours? Title? Then be prepared to bargain on the rest.

326. In many cases, the first offer is a fishing expedition. The company will go higher, offer more. They're just testing the waters.

327. Don't accept an offer on the spot, even if it contains everything you want. Ask for 24 to 48 hours to review the offer. You need time to prepare your negotiation strategy.

328. In preparation, write down what the company is looking for and how you more than meet those requirements. You'll need a finely honed sales pitch to ask for those extra dollars, perks, goodies.

329. Remember your biggest bargaining chip—the company's invested time and money in selecting you. They want to put the deal together and get on with more important things.

330. Know what you're worth in the market. Do your research. Then shoot for 10 to 20 percent more.

331. When asked about salary, include everything: base, bonuses (calculated on what you expect to receive if you meet your goals), savings plan contributions.

332. Worried the company might find out how much you made on your last job? Relax. Former companies rarely give out salary information.

333. Don't be afraid if the company says "no." They still want you. You just have to counter. If they're solid on the money, how about a bigger bonus, more vacation, a car? Be creative.

334. You're worth what you say you're worth. No one has *your* unique set of skills, personality, commitment. Don't sell yourself short.

335. You'll never have as much leverage as you do going into a company. Once inside, you become part of their compensation program with raises tied to variables out of your control.

336. Ask for more than you think you can get. Then there's room to negotiate. And be prepared to settle for what they counteroffer. Successful negotiation is about giving as well as getting.

337. Try to negotiate in person, never over the phone. It's much easier to wheel and deal face to face.

338. Always ask for a 90-day performance appraisal with salary increase built in.

339. Salary too low but you still want the job? Negotiate for other things: fewer hours, bigger title, more vacation. Always think in terms of the package, not its individual components.

340. Consider the law of averages: The final offer will be somewhere between what you ask for and what the initial offer is.

341. It's not over 'til it's over. Keep
interviewing until you accept the
offer. A deal can fall apart at the
last minute.

342. Get the offer in writing, accept in writing, and keep copies of all correspondence.

343. Know when to hold 'em, know when to fold 'em. Negotiate from a position of strength. Be prepared to walk away if your demands aren't met.

Parting
Words

344. There's no such thing as job security. But don't panic. Stay current on your skills and practice continual learning. Now, like never before, knowledge is power.

345. Think portability. You can take your skills anywhere. You're not defined by your title, function, field, or industry.

346. Forget career-long employment with one company. Think multiple employers, several careers, alternate workstyles, periodic self-employment.

347. You're only as good as your next gig. Keep your resume updated, your eyes and ears open for new opportunities. Learn everything you can from your company but always be prepared to move on.

348. Never give up. Rejection goes with the territory of looking for a job. Each "no" gets you that much closer to "yes."

349. The next time you get a rejection, remember: You can't be everyone's cup of tea, no matter how smart, capable, experienced, well-educated, or personable you are.

350. Getting a job isn't rocket science. It isn't brain surgery. But it does take time, effort, and commitment. You have what it takes to get any job you want. Believe in yourself.